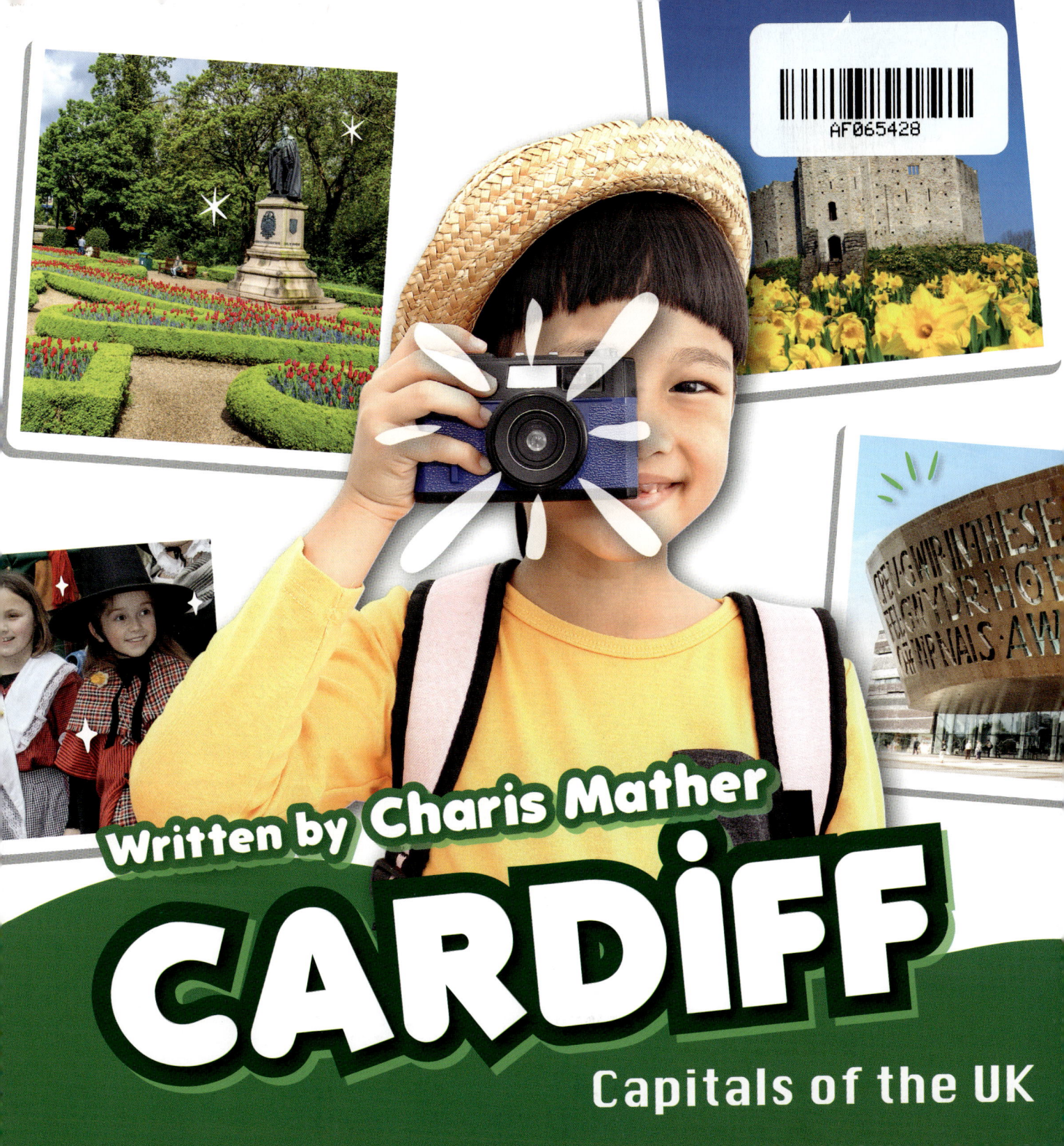

Written by Charis Mather

CARDIFF

Capitals of the UK

BookLife
PUBLISHING

©2024
BookLife Publishing Ltd.
King's Lynn, Norfolk
PE30 4LS, UK

All rights reserved.
Printed in India.

A catalogue record for this book is available from the British Library.

ISBN: 978-1-80505-610-2

Written by:
Charis Mather

Edited by:
Noah Leatherland

Designed by:
Amelia Harris

All facts, statistics, web addresses and URLs in this book were verified as valid and accurate at time of writing. No responsibility for any changes to external websites or references can be accepted by either the author or publisher.

Image Credits

All images are courtesy of Shutterstock.com, unless otherwise specified. With thanks to Getty Images, Thinkstock Photo and iStockphoto. Cover – Perfectorius, Warut Chinsai, Billy Stock, ComposedPix, Leonid Andronov, PNPImages. Recurring images – Nikolaeva, Voin_Sveta, ArtMari, Natasha Pankina, Liliana Danila. 2–3 – Lois GoBe. 4–5 – steved_np3, muratart, Maxger. 6–7 – Kalinin Ilya, Leonid Andronov, okili77. 8–9 – Billy Stock, Alexey Fedorenko. 10–11 – Billy Stock, National Library of Wales, Public domain via Wikimedia Commons, Seth Whales, CC BY-SA 4.0 via Wikimedia Commons. 12–13 – Chris De Bug, Richard Whitcombe, Gwens Graphic Studio, Daniel from Glasgow, United Kingdom, CC BY 2.0 via Wikimedia Commons. 14–15 – Billy Stock, Leonid Andronov, TR001, CC BY 3.0 via Wikimedia Commons. 16–17 – Billy Stock, Veronique Stone, jimmonkphotography. 18–19 – Aluna1, Bellamaree, Philip Bird LRPS CPAGB, Charlie Skinner. 20–21 – ComposedPix, Andreas Zerndl. 22–23 – Ray Morgan, Matthew Dixon, meunierd, RogerMechan.

CONTENTS

Page 4	Welcome to Cardiff!
Page 6	My Capital, My Country
Page 8	Castle Capital
Page 10	Old and Excellent
Page 12	Popular Places in the Present
Page 14	Outstanding Outdoors
Page 16	Much to Remember
Page 18	Buildings by the Bay
Page 20	City of Culture
Page 22	Only in Cardiff
Page 24	Glossary and Index

Words that look like this can be found in the glossary on page 24.

Welcome to Cardiff!

Welcome to Cardiff, my home city! If you have never been to Cardiff before, do not worry. I am here to introduce you to some of the most interesting and important places here.

I have taken loads of photos of my favourite spots in the city. I hope that you can learn a lot about Welsh <u>culture</u> and the history of Cardiff.

My Capital, My Country

Wales is part of a group of countries called the United Kingdom. The United Kingdom is made up of England, Wales, Scotland and Northern Ireland. Wales is to the west of England.

Scotland

Northern Ireland

England

Cardiff

Wales

Cardiff is the capital city of Wales. Capitals are where most of the big decisions in a country are made. Cardiff is home to more people than any other city in Wales.

Castle Capital

Cardiff has many well-known buildings, but it is most famous for its <u>medieval</u> castles. Many of the castles have fallen apart over time. Some, such as the Red Castle, are still standing.

The Red Castle

The Norman Keep in Cardiff Castle

Cardiff Castle is a famous medieval castle that is right in the middle of the city. Its long walls surround lots of old buildings. One building, the Norman keep, is on top of a small hill.

Old and Excellent

If you enjoy seeing very old places like Cardiff Castle, you could also go to Llandaff Cathedral. This church was built around 900 years ago.

Llandaff Cathedral now

Llandaff Cathedral around 240 years ago

Not far from Llandaff Cathedral is a place called the Bishop's Palace. Today, Bishop's Palace is mostly <u>ruins</u>. In medieval times, it was used as a home for some of Llandaff Cathedral's <u>clergy</u>.

Bishop's Palace

Popular Places in the Present

Cardiff has many well-known historical buildings, but it also has famous <u>modern</u> buildings. One of these is the Wales Millennium Centre. You can see lots of <u>performances</u> and art displays here.

The Centre has both English and Welsh writing on it.

Another modern building is the sports stadium, which many people visit to watch sports, including football and rugby. It can seat nearly 75,000 people!

Outstanding Outdoors

You can see Cardiff Castle from Bute Park.

Cardiff also has a large green area called Bute Park. Here, you can see a special tree garden, statues, a small stone circle and many other things as you walk around.

Flat Holm Island in the Bristol Channel

If you get a boat to the Bristol Channel, you can see Flat Holm Island. This small island is a great place to go on walks and learn more about Cardiff's history.

Much to Remember

Cardiff has lots of monuments. Monuments are structures or statues that are built to remind you of important people and events. Here are a few of the most interesting ones:

Welsh National War Memorial, Alexandra Gardens

The Merchant Seaman's Memorial remembers people who have been lost at sea.

This statue of Betty Campbell helps people remember how she helped make Cardiff more equal for everyone by teaching about Black history.

17

Buildings by the Bay

There are two rivers near the city that flow into an area called Cardiff Bay. Part of the bay is kept as a safe place for wild animals to live.

Lots of birds live here, including this heron.

Cardiff Bay is also home to the Pierhead Building. This red building was once important to Cardiff's coal <u>industry</u>. It now has a museum in it and is used for some important meetings and events.

There are lots of shops and places for activities around Cardiff Bay.

City of Culture

If you come to Cardiff at the right time, you might see people wearing traditional Welsh clothing. Some people dress up for the St David's Day Parade. This is a celebration of Wales's patron saint.

Another important celebration is National Eisteddfod. This is a huge celebration of the whole country's language, art, music and culture. It is held in a different place in Wales each year.

St David's Day and National Eisteddfod are celebrated all over Wales.

National Eisteddfod was celebrated at Cardiff Bay in 2018.

Only in Cardiff

You will not find any other place quite like Cardiff. I think it is amazing. Now that you have seen some of my favourite spots, hopefully you think so too!

There is so much more to see here. I cannot wait for you to explore my home city. When you visit, you will have to take your own photos of everything that I missed.

St Fagan's Museum

Cardiff City Hall

Statues on the Animal Wall near Cardiff Castle and Bute Park

Glossary

clergy	the people who work in a church
culture	the traditions, ideas and ways of life of a group of people
industry	a type of activity and business
medieval	the period of time from the 11th century to the 14th century
modern	to do with recent or present times
patron saint	a person who is believed by some to give special help to a person, place or activity
performances	shows put on to entertain people
ruins	buildings or structures that have fallen apart or broken down over time
traditional	to do with beliefs, customs or ways of behaving that have been around for a long time

Index

animals 18, 23
art 12, 21
castles 8–10, 14, 23
celebrations 20–21
churches 10
gardens 14, 16
hills 9
museums 19, 23
stadiums 13
statues 14, 16–17, 23